BRADFORD
OLD AND NEW

JANE & JOHN AYERS

Published by EP Publishing Limited 1976

This edition first published 1976 by
EP Publishing Limited,
East Ardsley, Wakefield, West Yorkshire,
England

ISBN 0 7158 1191 6

Please address all enquiries to EP Publishing Limited
(address as above)

Printed and bound in Great Britain by
G. Beard and Son Limited, Brighton, Sussex

Introduction

Before the end of the eighteenth century Bradford was a small town located in a textile area but with no particular claim to fame. Other local towns were more prosperous, as is indicated, for instance, by the Piece Hall in Halifax. Towards the end of the eighteenth century, however, the significance of the closely-situated coal seams and ironstone beds was realised, and when iron working was begun in the Low Moor area in 1779 it was the start of a great development in that industry on the south side of the town.

During the late eighteenth and early nineteenth centuries many innovations took place, leading to the mechanisation of most textile processes. With the advent of steam power to drive the new and ingenious machines Bradford was in a position of potential advantage, having readily available sources of coal and iron. This advantage was realised to the full, and Bradford began to flourish and to outstrip her neighbours.

Fortunately for Bradford, this source of industrial prosperity was coupled with another valuable raw material readily available near the town—beautiful honey-coloured building stone. Material of superb quality ideally suited for masonry was to be found to the north, and hard-wearing flagstones for paving to the south.

The St. George's Hall and the adjoining Milligan and Forbes warehouse (now the Telegraph and Argus building) were erected in 1853. During the next twenty-five years the centre of Bradford was completely transformed. Large, dignified, impressive industrial palaces replaced the former humble buildings. Almost overnight Bradford grew into a City.

Since 1875 fortunes in the textile trade have fluctuated. To listen to the woolmen themselves, one would gain the impression that turns were invariably for the worse. Sporadic development did take place during the next eighty years but the centre of the City was altered hardly at all.

Suddenly, almost a century after the first mushroom-like expansion, a second wave of demolition and rebuilding has occurred. Let us hope that these new buildings in Bradford will reflect the twentieth century as accurately as their Victorian predecessors speak to us of the nineteenth. Perhaps they do!

Many open spaces have been created during the process and it is our responsibility to ensure that these new urban oases become full of trees and green places which are pleasant for the people to be in as well as providing dignified civic areas.

City centres throughout the world have been adapted to cope with ever-increasing traffic and Bradford is no exception. But we must always remember that cities are primarily for people and not for cars. The prairie-like wide open spaces across the dual carriageways strike terror into the hearts of all but the most intrepid pedestrians. This may be good for traffic circulation, but is it good for our cities—or for us?

No praise would be too high for our photographers, Messrs. C. H. Wood. They have taken full advantage of the best summer we have enjoyed since records began to produce some sparkling photographs. Enormous enthusiasm was developed for this venture and the greatest care has been exercised in ensuring that the new pictures are, as nearly as possible, along exactly the same alignments as the earlier ones. In one pair of pictures the clock even shows exactly the same time, forty-five years later.

The old photographs were collected from a variety of sources but we would particularly wish to thank the staff of the local history section of the Bradford Central Library and of the Telegraph and Argus Library for their co-operation and help. We are also very much indebted to the scholarship and generous help of John S. Roberts, a friend whom we respect equally for his character and for his knowledge of all aspects of Bradford history.

Finally, we both wish to say how we have enjoyed this joint venture; we hope that this brief look at Bradford past and present gives our readers as much pleasure as it has given us in compiling it.

Jane and John Ayers
Bradford, 1976

Contents

Town Hall Square - c. 1890
Carved in Carrara marble, surmounted by
an elaborate neo-Gothic canopy and
protected by superb wrought-iron railings,
Sir Titus Salt gazes with quiet dignity
towards Saltaire. After only twenty-two
years in this important setting his statue
was moved in 1896 to sit rather
incongruously amongst the trees in Lister
Park.

1

Town Hall Square - 1975
Trees now grace the city centre where steam trams used to run. The recently-completed Police Headquarters, like the rest of us, can only reflect on the glories of an earlier age. In the foreground modern street furniture, pop-eyed but sinister, regards all that takes place like a rectangular robot.

Market Street from Town Hall Square - c. 1880
The curved façade of the former Provincial Building Society built in 1871 leads gently into the sweep of Market Street beyond. The newly-completed Swan Arcade (1878) can be seen in the distance. All the buildings between it and the Salt statue have been replaced. The cab drivers have attitudes of elegant relaxation which would be quite impossible in a modern taxi.

Market Street from Town Hall Square - 1975
Only the Bradford and District Bank (with the pointed dome in the distance), built in 1873, remains on that side of Market Street. Notice how we are beset by signs and road markings telling us where we should turn, how we should cross, where we may wait, where we must not wait, what we must on no account do, and exactly where we certainly should not be doing it.

4

Town Hall Square from Thornton Road - c. 1895
Already the space in front of the Town Hall, previously open, is being encroached upon. Metal tracks and steam trams have appeared. Lockwood and Mawson's Town Hall stands as it was originally built before Norman Shaw's extensions in 1905. In the distance is a rare view along the bottom of Leeds Road.

5

City Hall from Thornton Road - 1975
Once again we are getting an open space. We can see that green grass and trees will grow in the city centre. Here is a wonderful opportunity to create a spacious and dignified civic area; gardens and walking areas have already been created on both sides of the road and there are plans to join them together—let us hope that these plans are carried out soon.

Town Hall Street from Thornton Road - c. 1895
Opposite stands Chapel Lane Unitarian
Chapel, designed by Andrews and Pepper
and built in 1868. Contrast in transport is
seen between the horse-drawn cart and
the steam tram returning to Bradford
centre from a journey up Manchester
Road. It appears that being marooned on
traffic islands has been a problem for
pedestrians for longer than we might
imagine.

Towards the Law Courts from Thornton Road - 1975
Trees are in leaf, roses are in bloom and the fountains play in the centre of Bradford. The recently-cleaned extension to the City Hall built in 1905 contrasts well with the new Law Courts completed in 1972, but beyond we see the unrelenting horizontals of the multi-storey car park, and the rapidly-growing transport interchange.

Market Street, towards Forster Square - 1897
No expense has been spared to decorate Market Street with flags and bunting to celebrate Queen Victoria's Diamond Jubilee. Every available flagpole and lamp-post has been called into service. The Swan Arcade scowls darkly across the street towards the Wool Exchange on the left. The clothes worn by people in the street form an interesting study, especially when compared with the same scene opposite.

Market Street, towards Cheapside - 1975
The Wool Exchange and the characteristic dome of the Bradford District Bank remain, but Arndale House, clad in Portland stone, stands on the site of the Swan Arcade. Beyond these, Market Street has been shortened and the near-moribund Midland Station masked from view by an undistinguished office block.

Market Street, towards Town Hall Square - 1897
This is the opposite view along Market Street from those in Plates 9 and 10, again on the occasion of the Diamond Jubilee. In the right foreground can be seen the Boar's Head, lavishly garlanded with flowers. The many brewers' carts indicate that the festivities took forms other than mere decoration. Beyond, on the right, is the Bradford Old Bank, designed by Alfred Waterhouse and completed in 1867.

11

Market Street, towards Town Hall Square - 1975
The modern replacement of Waterhouse's Bank is seen in the right foreground. Opposite, the beautiful stone and meticulous detailing of the Bradford District Bank, built in 1873, stand out clearly in the evening sunshine. Islands studded with traffic lights and bollards relieve the monotony of the sea of tarmacadam.

Morley Street, towards Town Hall Square - c. 1955
Although at the time of this photograph the island was negotiated by trolley buses, in earlier times less manoeuvrable trams had a private and privileged route straight through the middle of it. With the exception of the Town Hall itself, all the buildings in the foreground of this view were soon to be demolished, and the street pattern completely changed.

Odeon 1 and 2, towards Town Hall Square - 1975
The angle of view has been slightly changed so that the clock tower of the Town Hall, now City Hall, can be included. Although neatly detailed and sensitively proportioned, the Provincial Building Society, in a profoundly symbolic way, dominates all its neighbours.

Junction of Morley Street and Little Horton Lane - 1904
On May 4th 1904, in the presence of seventy thousand onlookers, the statue of Queen Victoria was unveiled by her grandson, the Prince of Wales, accompanied by Princess Mary. Here we see the crowds at ten to two on that day. Although not a lot can be seen of complete outfits, there is a good selection of best hats on view.

Junction of Morley Street and Little Horton Lane - 1975
The shadow of the cenotaph in the foreground indicates that the photographer has his back to Queen Victoria's statue. Here we can see clearly the change of scale that takes place when a city is adapted for motor traffic. The cold baldness of this view contrasts with the intimate bustle of the last.

16

Tyrrel Street from bottom of Manchester Road - c. 1957
Although this photograph was taken only relatively recently, most of the buildings seen here have since been demolished. Collinson's Cafe and Burton's the tailors can be picked out along Tyrrel Street, to the left. The island block, containing the Mechanics Institute and the old Provincial Building Society, is seen in the centre. To the right, demolition has taken place to make way for Thornton House.

Police Headquarters, towards Tyrrel Street - 1975
Almost a century in time separates the Provincial Building Society block on the left (1970) and the Town Hall on the right (1873). What tremendous changes have taken place in social attitudes and living standards, as well as in the architect's concept of beauty in building, during that time!

Chapel Lane Chapel - c. 1967
Built in 1865 to designs by Andrews and Pepper, Chapel Lane Chapel stands marooned in a sea of demolition, and was destined itself to be taken down shortly afterwards.

Bradford City Law Courts - 1975

On a site previously devoted to the dissemination of the Laws of God stands a building dedicated to the implementation of the Laws of the Land. Simple and dignified and perfectly appropriate to its function, the Law Courts is one of the best modern buildings in the city. To the left is Norman Shaw's imposing façade of the Town Hall extension (1905).

Town Hall Square - c. 1948

The number three tram from Queensbury is just returning to the terminus in Tyrrel Street. The open ends of the upper deck were always very popular with schoolboys. Unfortunately, the schoolboys were not usually so popular with the other passengers—especially in winter! Across the crowded and busy square it can be seen that it is five to three (Guinness Mean Time).

Town Hall Square - 1975
Notice how much clearer overhead is the view without tram wires and all the necessary supports. There is a much greater sense of space in front of the Town Hall after the removal of the Mechanics Institute, and the façades of the buildings opposite can be appreciated from across the square.

Bridge Street - c. 1880
The site for this block of buildings was auctioned in 1870. A condition of the sale was that the buildings erected on the site should be equal in quality and character and of similar height to those built by Messrs. Brown, Muff and Co. Ltd. on an adjacent plot and completed that year.

Bridge Street - 1975
That the conditions imposed at the auction of the site were satisfied can be clearly seen. The buildings, remarkably unchanged over the years, show a lightness of touch and a delicacy of detail which is rare in Victorian Bradford. The one with iron cresting at eaves level is particularly fine.

Bottom of Leeds Road - c. 1955
Not all the old buildings in Bradford were good! This undistinguished group of offices and warehouses between Leeds Road and Market Street was taken down in 1957. These were poor buildings for an important city centre site.

25

Bottom of Leeds Road - 1975

The effective use of a curved elevation to take maximum advantage of a central site is seen here in Thornton House, completed in 1959. This was Bradford's introduction to glass-sided buildings. Marked changes in the styling of motor vehicles have clearly taken place over the intervening twenty years.

Bowling Green Hotel, Bridge Street - c. 1865
Rebuilt in 1750 in place of an earlier seventeenth-century building, the Bowling Green was for many years the best inn of the town. Through the years the space in front of this hotel was used for political and religious meetings, and the famous coach 'Rockingham Bob', with four horses in hand, drove up to its very windows. In 1871 the Mechanics Institute was built on this site.

Provincial Building Society - 1975
Originally built in 1970 and extended in 1975, this glistening cream-coloured office block dominates the city centre. Although not enormous by modern standards it certainly represents a marked change in scale, when compared with earlier buildings. The Refuge Building on the right was built c. 1880.

Bridge Street - c. 1860
The modest buildings standing in the middle of Bradford are well illustrated in this photograph of the horse and cattle fair which was held twice yearly in Bridge Street. The Bowling Green Inn stood nearby to the right. In the distance can be seen the square form of the St. George's Hall. The site for the Victoria Hotel (built in 1867) lies beyond.

Bridge Street - 1975
Between 1865 and 1885 this part of the city centre was completely transformed. The St. George's Hall, built in 1853, is the only building still surviving from the earlier photograph. Enormous changes have taken place in modes of transport, in fashion and in civic atmosphere.

Market Street - c. 1900
A succession of fine Victorian buildings stands on the left hand side of Market Street. The Wool Exchange, completed in 1867 to designs by Lockwood and Mawson, is in the Gothic revival style. Then follows the Parkinson Building (1877), the Bradford Old Bank (1867) and the Boar's Head Hotel. Closing the view is the curtain wall to the Forster Square Station.

Market Street - 1975

The quality of Victorian craftsmanship and the durability of the local stone are clearly seen in the Wool Exchange, now more than a hundred years old. It is interesting to compare the lamp standards of 1900 with those of 1975. One is left to conjecture whether standards have gone up or down!

Sunbridge Road - c. 1925

An Act of Parliament, dated 1873, gave the Corporation powers to construct a new road from the site of the ancient Sun Bridge westwards. This relieved congestion on Thornton Road and at the same time enabled much old and inferior property to be demolished. Building continued along this fine thoroughfare until the First World War.

33

Sunbridge Road - 1975
It is an instructive lesson in atmosphere to notice the complete change in character which has taken place in fifty years.
This is caused only by a different road surface, redesigned shop fronts, modern vehicles and up-to-date clothes. The
buildings are virtually identical in the two photographs.

Tyrrel Street - c. 1900
The Bradfordians of 1900 certainly set high standards in personal dress. The taxi cabs are very well turned out too!
The building on the left belonged to George Thorpe and Co., a firm of outfitters and house furnishers, whilst opposite,
Brown, Muff and Co. had not yet taken over the building which is marked 'To Let'. On the corner of Bank Street the
Bradford branch of the Yorkshire Banking Co. still stands.

Tyrrel Street - 1975
With the exception of the Yorkshire Banking Co., which has been rebuilt and incorporated into Brown, Muff and Co., all the buildings remain and they have all been cleaned, revealing the beautiful honey-coloured local stone. The haphazard accumulation of extensions above roof level creates an untidy and slightly disturbing effect.

Ivegate - c. 1920
Along with Westgate and Kirkgate,
Ivegate is one of the original thoroughfares
of the town. Leading as it did from the old
market cross, which stood at the junction
of Westgate and Kirkgate, down the hill to
the Sun Bridge, it was an important route
across the Thornton beck and towards the
south-east. The Sun Inn, well-known in
coaching days, stood on the site of the
present Prudential building.

Ivegate - 1975
The street still retains the character which makes the city centre so interesting to walk around. The age-long history of the narrow steep ascent can be appreciated to this day. Now that alternative routes more suitable for motor vehicles have been made, Ivegate would make a most attractive pedestrian area.

Junction of Kirkgate and Ivegate - c. 1860
Before 1800 this was the centre of Bradford. The market cross stood close by. The important road to the church, Kirkgate, curves interestingly away to the left. Only thirty yards along Kirkgate stood the manor house erected in 1705. A good idea of the pre-Victorian quality of Bradford can be gained from this photograph.

39

Junction of Kirkgate and Ivegate - 1975
Although at first sight this junction now looks very different, much remains from the earlier photograph. The architectural character of the buildings has been considerably changed by applied surface finishes, alterations to window patterns and up-to-date though sometimes insensitive shop fronts.

Kirkgate from Westgate - c. 1875
The elegant premises occupied by Manoah Rhodes and Son stood opposite the top of Ivegate. The shop appears to have a tremendous range of silver trays, bowls and candelabra. The firm later occupied the block between Queensgate and Bank Street. Farther along Kirkgate can be seen the turret of the Kirkgate market built in 1871 on a site previously occupied by the manor house.

41

Kirkgate from Westgate - 1975
Setting a new scale and establishing a completely different character is the new Kirkgate market complex. Gaunt and heavy-looking ribbed concrete slabs rise high above the narrow street.

Kirkgate, Darley Street crossing - c. 1875
In the centre stands the building erected for the Bradford Banking Co. in 1858. A strong contribution to the quality of the street scene is provided by the heavy railings round the bank and the distinctive lamp standards. The dog, the symbol of the Talbot Hotel, can just be discerned, past the lamps to the right of the photograph, outside the old building prior to the erection of new premises in 1878.

Kirkgate, Darley Street crossing - 1975
It is quite entertaining to observe the changes which have taken place on the Bank building during 100 years. The new Kirkgate Market building, under construction, contrasts markedly with its predecessor built in 1871. The Talbot Hotel, much more distinguished than the earlier one, can be seen on the right just beyond the block erected for Manoah Rhodes.

Darley Street, looking uphill - c. 1895
This view gives a very clear indication of the quality of streetscape to be seen in Bradford at the end of the last century. Fine, carefully-carved local stone encases the Kirkgate market, with the library beyond. The numerous signs and busy-looking frontages indicate the development of a flourishing shopping area.

Darley Street, looking uphill - 1975
Darley Street remains a shopping street attracting pedestrians in great numbers. It seems strange that even though flatter streets exist in the city, this steeply-sloping one is still popular with shoppers. Dress in 1975 appears to be much more varied than in 1890. The bank in the right foreground is unaltered, as is the building beyond it, but elsewhere in the street many changes have taken place.

Looking down Darley Street - c. 1948

Darley Street looks very busy in this scene. The Savoy cinema on the left is now almost forgotten, and the style of the lettering on shop fronts, the shapes of the motor cars and the road surface of granite setts all appear surprisingly old-fashioned. Women's skirts were much more generous than in the preceding years as cloth became more easily available after the scarcities of wartime.

Looking down Darley Street - 1975
The new Kirkgate development, partly because of its simpler architectural treatment and partly because of its greater height, makes Darley Street appear narrower. The same effect can be seen in the uphill views. Notice how the photographer has even ensured that the traffic light still shines green!

48

Bottom of Cheapside - c. 1935
The rain glistening on the road surface and the misty, almost murky atmosphere will be sights remembered by many older Bradfordians. On the right is Beckett's Bank, built in 1885 and still standing. Beyond is the Bradford Old Bank designed by Alfred Waterhouse and demolished about 1937. Farther beyond and barely visible is the Bradford District Bank, completed in 1873.

Bottom of Cheapside - 1975

Alongside Beckett's Bank the modern lamp-post bows towards the Portland stone developments of the 1960s. Milnes and France's beautiful bank, built so solidly of local stone and once the epitome of Victorian prosperity, now stands rather incongruously amongst modern buildings faced with alien materials. The Midland Hotel, with its intricate iron balustrading, was built in 1885.

Forster Square - c. 1925

The Cathedral can be seen above the roof of the General Post Office, which was built in 1887 to a design by Sir Henry Tanner. The building is designed in the style of a French chateau, with pavilions at each end. Street name plates, shop signs and lamp standards are worthy of study.

Bottom of Cheapside, towards Forster Square - 1975
The complete realignment of the entry into Forster Square can be appreciated by comparing this view with the last.
Slab-sided office blocks close the view to the Cathedral and the Post Office which, sadly, is destined to be taken down
to improve traffic circulation. The new dual carriageway leads mysteriously round the corner. On the balcony of the
Midland Hotel hangs a discreet but none the less ominous 'To Let' sign. Is this the first stage of further development?

Bottom of Cheapside, looking up - c. 1880
The round-headed doorway and overhanging oriel window of the Bradford Old Bank appear in the left foreground. The recently-completed Boar's Head in the centre forms an impressive block. The prospect of supporting the upper two stories for years ahead does not seem to appeal to the carved heads on the first floor stage. Behind stand the old station and the predecessor to the Midland Hotel.

53

Bottom of Cheapside, looking up - 1975
Started just before the Second World War and completed soon after it, the new building for Barclays Bank affords an opportunity for comparison with the earlier one on the same site. The Boar's Head has gone, revealing the Midland Hotel of 1885. The attractive original zinc covering to the cupola has been replaced by roofing felt. The curtain wall of the Forster Square station is hidden by curtain walling of a century later.

Forster Square, towards Cathedral - c. 1930
A tram of the period waits in Forster Square to depart for Baildon Bridge. In front of the General Post Office, built in 1887 on the lines of a French chateau, stands the statue to W. E. Forster, the pioneer of the 1870 Education Act which led to the erection of numerous schools in Bradford and throughout the country.

Forster Square, towards Cathedral - 1975
The statue of Forster no longer stands in the centre of the square named after him. He has been moved from the main traffic island to a narrow peninsula between Canal Road and Bolton Road. The photographer saw to it that the Post Office clock shows exactly the same time, but compare the Bradford metro public service vehicle with its counterpart of 45 years ago.

Forster Square - 1910

We can see that in 1910 enormous efforts were made to celebrate the coronation of George V. One gets the impression that the corporation transport department were exhibiting their whole fleet for the occasion. Despite the gaiety of the bunting and the holiday atmosphere, the buildings stand behind looking very grim and black long before the days of stone cleaning.

Forster Square - 1975
Nothing that can be seen in the previous photographs, the buildings, the roads, the bus shelters or the traffic islands, remains to be seen in 1975. All is either new or newly revealed to view. The island in the foreground is a pleasant oasis in a rather barren desert of stone, glass and concrete—but it is necessary to burrow underground in order to reach it!

Forster Square, towards Well Street - c. 1950

The dark, powerful and imposing warehouses which had dominated the area of Bradford around Well Street, Leeds Road and Vicar Lane since the 1860s were beginning to succumb to changes in trade and economy. One of them has already been demolished by the time of this photograph, and the rest were to follow.

Forster Square, towards Well Street - 1975
Gone is the impressive curving façade of Sir Jacob Behren's warehouse. Gone are the blocks between Swaine Street and Broadway. Only the old BDA building remains, but it is still a fine and impressive building after recent cleaning. Central House, clad in stone from Portland and marble from Italy, is mercifully unaware of its Bradford sandstone forebears.

Midland Railway Station - c. 1860
These station buildings for the Midland Railway were swept away when the station was rebuilt and extended in the 1880s. The style is similar to a country house with a central block, wings and pavilions. Even the drive curves elegantly beneath the glazed canopy where passengers could dismount protected from the weather. At the left a simple warehouse survives from the large number that stood in Bermondsey. Posters advertise visits to places as exotic as Australia, Canada, New York and Birmingham.

61

Midland Railway Station - 1975
The disfigured remnants of what was originally a covered yard stand beneath the graceful façade of the Midland Hotel, built in 1885. The station concourse beyond has been completely re-roofed. The large and impressive warehouses at the end of Canal Road, enhanced by cleaning, can be seen in the distance, and rows of terrace houses climb the hillside beyond.

MIDLAND RAILWAY STATION, BRADFORD.

Forster Square, Midland Hotel - c. 1890
From atop his granite pedestal Richard Oastler silently admonishes the residents of the palatial new Midland Hotel for their lack of awareness of social inequality. The new station complex and curtain wall are very impressive. Cab drivers wait patiently at Oastler's feet for any potential fares. Notice the superb horse and cart walking briskly out of the right of the picture.

63

Forster Square, Midland Hotel - 1975
Although still impressive in the amount of craftsmanship lavished upon it and the care with which the stonework details were designed, the curtain wall has lost dignity by the absence of the polygonal turret at the right hand end. The architectural effect of the station wall itself with its chimney stacks and balustrades is missed. Sleek gleaming cars replace the sturdy glistening horses of an earlier era.

Midland Station interior - c. 1900
In accordance with normal Victorian practice the station shed is roofed over, containing the steam and echoing the noise of the engines. Remember that the atmosphere of a Victorian station would be as tense as that of an airport departure lounge today. Everyone in this picture seems stiffly aware of the camera.

65

Midland Station interior - 1975
Its days as a passenger station almost over, the simple functional concourse is resigned to its duties of handling parcels and packages. Beyond, the platforms only are roofed over to protect the now-absent passengers, leaving the rolling stock exposed to the weather. The only person visible in the station could not care less about the photographer!

Cathedral and Church Bank - c. 1885

The Cathedral, originally Bradford Parish Church and characteristic of its area and period, stands high on the hillside above Forster Square. Church Bank is seen to be a very narrow cobbled street, little more than an alleyway. Roof tops and chimney stacks are haphazardly jumbled together around the church steps which led steeply up to the church. The scale of older Bradford is seen on the right beyond the new and impressive warehouse.

Cathedral and Church Bank - 1975
The Post Office by Sir Henry Tanner stands at the foot of a widened but still steep Church Bank. The original church has been altered and extended in recognition of its status as a Cathedral. From this viewpoint the multi-storey blocks of flats stacked cheek by jowl behind the church reduce the scale of the church tower.

Peel Square - 1862
The unbelievably ornate and elaborate curving façade of home trade warehouses built for Messrs. Tetley and Abercrombie in 1862 was designed by Milnes and France, who were responsible for many imposing warehouses in Leeds Road and Vicar Lane. The bronze likeness of Robert Peel, the first statue to be erected in Bradford, was unveiled in 1855. He is standing in an appropriately modest and appreciative attitude.

Hall Ings and Charles Street - 1975
Peel Square has gone. Peel himself has gone, banished to an early retirement amidst sequestered shade in the park which bears his name. In their place we can see the wide open spaces of Hall Ings, modified to suit the needs of modern traffic. The elaborate dome of the magnificent Law-Russell warehouse in Vicar Lane can be seen peeping coyly over the distant rooftops.

St. George's Hall - c. 1890

What a massive, elegant and impressive building this must have appeared to the Bradfordians of 1853 when it was first opened. It was indeed a bold initiative to venture upon a concert hall of these dimensions before Bradford really began to boom. With the exception of the late Gothic Cathedral, this is now the oldest building in the City Centre. The Telegraph and Argus building, built originally as a home trade warehouse, was also completed in 1853.

St. George's Hall - 1975
The removal of the older property and its replacement in the 1930s by the Britannia House, seen on the left, has led to a more open view of the St. George's Hall. The Milligan and Forbes warehouse adjacent, which is designed like an Italian palazzo, maintains the scale and classical derivation of the St. George's Hall. Farther along Hall Ings was the even purer Greek revival Court House of 1832. The Gothic revival had not yet begun.

Charles Street, towards Peel Square - c. 1925
Beautifully capturing the mood set by the granite setts, metal kerbs and tall dark buildings, this view of one of the minor streets in the city shows us clearly the character of central Bradford as it used to be. Old and new methods of traction stand on opposite sides of the street. The sandwich board man reminds us that commercial breaks, in one form or another, have been with us for longer than we might imagine.

Charles Street, towards Hall Ings - 1975
What a transformation has taken place! Nothing except the street line of the former photograph remains. The buildings are cleaner and neater and more crisp in their details and consequently the character of the street has changed. Our whole lives are lived in cleaner and neater surroundings than fifty years ago—but are they better?

Victoria Square - 1904
Standing proudly above a frothy sea of elegant millinery (just look at those hats!), Victoria appears unmoved by all the tremendous celebrations that were going on at her feet. Seventy thousand people witnessed the unveiling of this fine bronze statue by her grandson, then Prince of Wales. Behind stands the Horton Lane Congregational Chapel, the so-called Cathedral of Nonconformity, where many men of great influence in Bradford worshipped.

Victoria Square - 1975
It is strange that this is the only statue in the city centre which still stands in its original position. The setting, though bedecked with roses, is somehow less impressive, less civic, now that the fine building behind has gone. Although it is not apparent at first sight, the Queen now stands on a traffic island, a fate shared by Oastler, Peel, Forster and Salt before their removal was thought necessary.

Rawson Square - c. 1960
Richard Oastler, the tireless pioneer for shorter hours in the mills for children and women, stands in Rawson Square where he was moved to in 1920 from his original position in Forster Square. Wedged as he is between the Rawson Hotel and the Unity Hall and surrounded by a plethora of urban street litter (traffic lights, control boxes, bollards, grit boxes, telephone boxes, public toilets and road signs), he tries to maintain his dignity.

Rawson Square - 1975
Oastler's statue has been moved once again, this time into a quieter but less noticeable position in Northgate, where he is surrounded by flower beds and benches. The buildings through the gap have changed but the Square itself retains some of its character. Note the improvements in amenity by having the two telephone boxes standing north-south instead of east-west as previously.

James Gate - 1930s
An odd and interesting narrow corner of old Bradford, its character set by the stone paving, the Shap granite kerb stones and the cobbles in the street as much as by the irregular lines of the crumbling staircase and the lamp-post beyond.

James Gate - 1975

Although the main line of the street remains, much of its interest has gone. It looks quite respectable! There is clearly nothing to fear round the next corner. The covering of the road surface with tarmacadam has changed the character of this old corner, but it is easier to walk on. Perhaps the young lady in her platform shoes is grateful for that!

Cheapside/Duke Street - c. 1955

This humble warehouse, reduced to the simplest building elements, was depicted by Crichton in one of his beautiful water colours during the 1870s. It changed hardly at all between then and 1955, only the hoist housing at roof level having been removed. In the first half of the nineteenth century the warehousing area of Bermondsey stood opposite, but was later swept away by the railway.

Cheapside/Duke Street - 1975
The modern shops and offices now standing on this site, although not built quite so sturdily, have a lightness and airiness that is a relief from the dark oppressive piles of the last century. The staggered frontages and young trees are beginning to produce an urban atmosphere which is new to Bradford.

North Parade - c. 1875
A cab waits patiently outside the
neo-Gothic Church Institute, completed in
1873. Across the end of the street stands
Christ Church. It is difficult to believe that
when it was built in 1815 this church
stood in a semi-rural setting. It was
demolished in 1879 to make a new route
out of Bradford via Darley Street.

North Parade - 1975

The former sense of quiet seclusion has gone and the Church Institute now stands alongside a busy main thoroughfare. It will be seen that despite this the buildings are virtually unchanged, though insensitive shop fitting has changed the architectural character of the Church Institute at ground floor level, as with so many other buildings in Bradford.

Manningham Lane, Theatre Royal - c. 1880
The theatre was originally opened as the Royal Alexandra in 1864 to designs by Andrews and Pepper. Its name was changed to Theatre Royal five years later. Sir Henry Irving gave his last performance in this theatre, dying later the same evening. The heavy-wheeled horse transport plods steadily towards the centre of the town.

Manningham Lane, Royal Cinema - 1975
Although it has been considerably modified, the Royal Cinema is still just recognisable as the original Theatre Royal. Many of the other buildings in the view remain the same as almost a hundred years ago. Modern transport vehicles are making the same journey towards the city centre.

Manningham Lane, towards North Parade - c. 1930
Fashions form an interesting comparison in these two views. It is almost startling to see how taste has changed in clothing styles, motor cars, motor bicycles and even theatre frontages. The dome of the old Regent Cinema can be seen on the right beyond Busby's, which occupied only half of the present block. The Yorkshire Penny Bank looks grimy beyond the tramcar.

Manningham Lane, towards North Parade - 1975
Messrs. Busby's premises have been skilfully extended so as to appear to be a unified frontage, and the name has changed to Debenham's. The cleaned Yorkshire Bank, designed by James Ledingham and built in 1895, enables the very elaborate Queen Anne style of architecture to be more clearly seen and consequently better appreciated.

Manningham Lane - c. 1880

This was the prestige approach to the town. Large impressive residences—they were clearly far more than just houses —peep out from behind the trees. The epitome of all Victorian nannies wheels out baby in an extremely aristocratic pram. A beautiful carriage and pair trots elegantly by—although it does appear to be hogging the centre of the road slightly!

Manningham Lane - 1975

Although this is still an impressive tree-lined route, many of the large houses are now subdivided into flats or used as offices. The residential areas have moved farther away from the centre of the city. Smoother, faster vehicles glide over the modern tarmacadam surface. The baby carriage on the right is seen to be a much simpler, more functional piece of equipment than its Victorian predecessor.

Primrose Terrace, off Green Lane - c. 1960
The rather stark atmosphere of a stone-built terrace of houses with stone boundary walls and stone-paved street and causeways is clearly seen in this view. Some acknowledgement of architectural design is seen in the door heads and carved gate posts. The old gas lamps remain, although long outdated.

St. Patrick's School - 1975
That this photograph is taken exactly along the line of the previous one can be confirmed by checking the relative positions of All Saints Church spire and two nearby chimneys (left centre). Primrose Terrace and two adjacent streets have disappeared and have been replaced by a modern school. The ever-growing University campus can be seen on the hillside beyond.

Promenade, Bowling Park - c. 1885
Bowling Park was opened in September 1880 by the Mayor, Angus Holden, and was one of a fine series of parks situated around the town; Peel Park and Lister Park were opened in the 1860s and Horton Park in the 1870s. Although rather naked and new-looking, the promenade is clearly popular and was later to become one of the places to be seen on Sunday afternoons. To judge from this view, however, Victorian women seem to have had no time for such pleasures!

93

Promenade, Bowling Park - 1975
Although there have been some changes in level the main lines of the promenade are seen to be little changed. The trees have matured splendidly, providing the required atmosphere and background for an established park. Habits have changed over the years and Bradfordians are now more likely to be found in Scarborough or Morecambe on a Bank Holiday than in Bowling Park.

Barkerend Improvement Scheme: Before - 1972
Curzon Road, typical of many streets selected for improvement in the area of Barkerend Road, is over-wide, paved with sandstone cobbles and bounded by flagged pavements. The houses are begrimed with the effects of atmospheric pollution and the whole scene has an empty and depressing atmosphere.

Barkerend Improvement Scheme: After - 1975
The houses have been cleaned and maintained, the carriageway has been surfaced with smooth tarmacadam and grass verges planted with trees have been introduced. A much pleasanter aspect has been created. This was a bold venture by the Local Authority to improve an existing area rather than replace it, and the experiment has been very successful.

Cemetery Road, looking east - c. 1935
This view, taken in the 1930s, depicts the appearance of Bradford from Cemetery Road looking east. Myriads of chimneys pierce the gloomy sky and from most of them pours a great pall of evil smoke. A large part of Bradford looked very much like this at the time. Note the two fine chimneys originally standing alongside Princeville Road.

Cemetery Road, looking east - 1975
Many of the chimneys have disappeared and those that remain emit little smoke. The whole city has a much cleaner and fresher look. Smokeless zones have served their purpose in eliminating not only industrial smoke but also that from domestic chimneys. It is now worthwhile to clean the city's buildings.